SUPER SILLY JOKES
FOR 7+ YEAR OLDS

www.juniorscholars.club

LIKE PUZZLES?

AVAILABLE ON OUR AMAZON STORE

KNOCK, KNOCK!
WHO'S THERE?
LETTUCE
LETTUCE WHO?
LETTUCE IN, IT'S COLD OUT HERE!

WHY DID THE BIRDIE GO TO THE PARTY?

TO PECK UP SOME CHIPS AND DIP

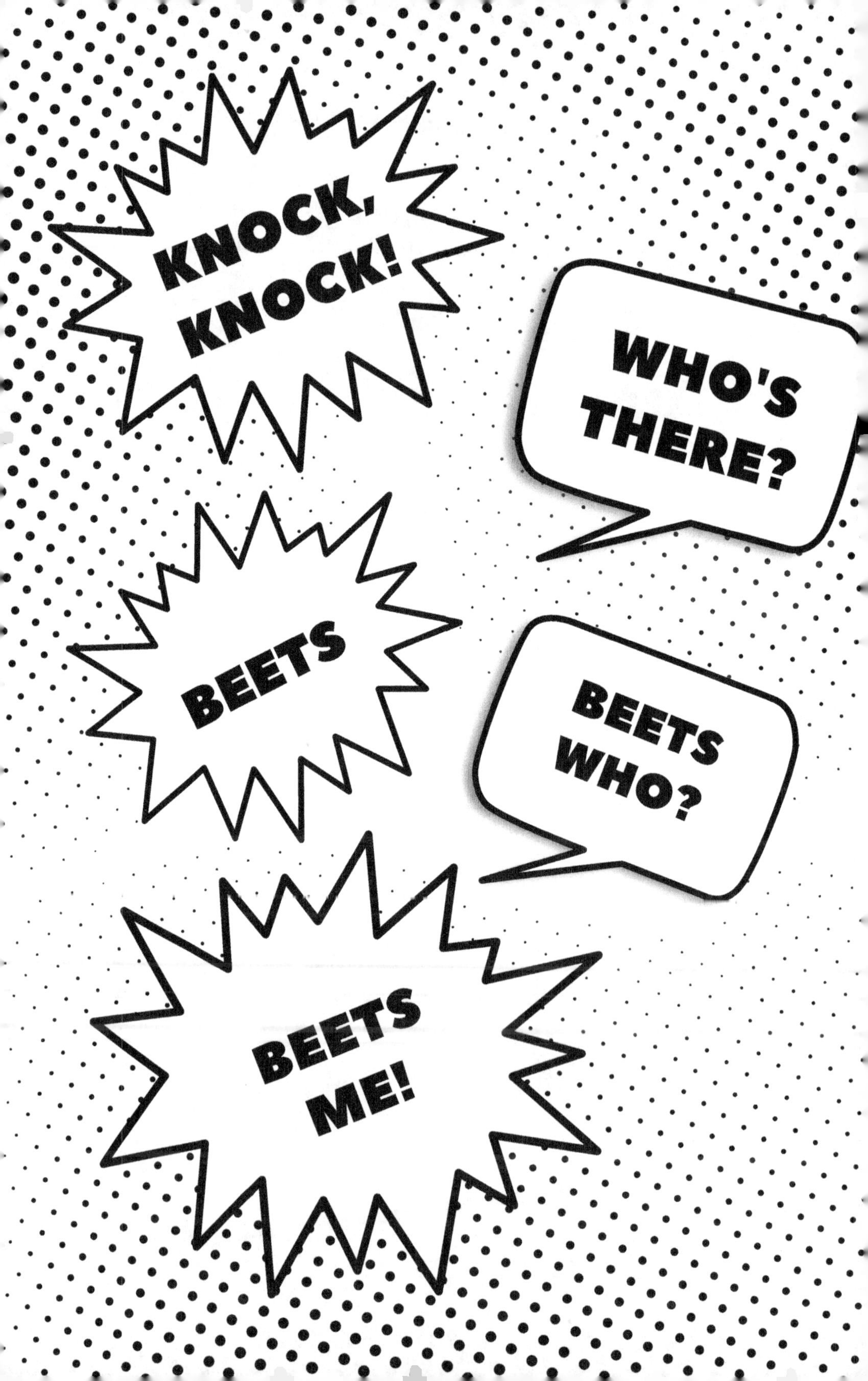
KNOCK, KNOCK!
WHO'S THERE?
BEETS
BEETS WHO?
BEETS ME!

KNOCK, KNOCK!
WHO'S THERE?
WEEKEND
WEEKEND WHO?
WEEKEND DO ANYTHING WE WANT!

KNOCK, KNOCK!
WHO'S THERE?
WITCHES
WITCHES WHO?
WITCHES THE BEST WAY OUT OF THIS NEIGHBORHOOD!?

KNOCK, KNOCK!
WHO'S THERE?
WENDY
WENDY WHO?
WENDY BELL GONNA START WORKING AGAIN?

KNOCK, KNOCK!
WHO'S THERE?
WATER
WATER WHO?
WATER YOU ASKING SO MANY QUESTIONS FOR, JUST OPEN UP!

KNOCK, KNOCK!
WHO'S THERE?
THEODORE
THEODORE WHO?
THEODORE WASN'T OPENED SO I KNOCKED

WHAT'S A PIRATE'S FAVORITE CLASS TO TAKE IN SCHOOL?

ARRRRT

KNOCK, KNOCK!
WHO'S THERE?
LENA
LENA WHO?
LENA LITTLE CLOSER AND I'LL TELL YOU!

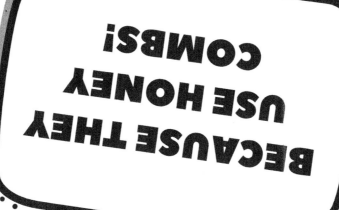

KNOCK, KNOCK!
WHO'S THERE?
NEEDLE
NEEDLE WHO?
NEEDLE LITTLE HELP OPENING THE DOOR!

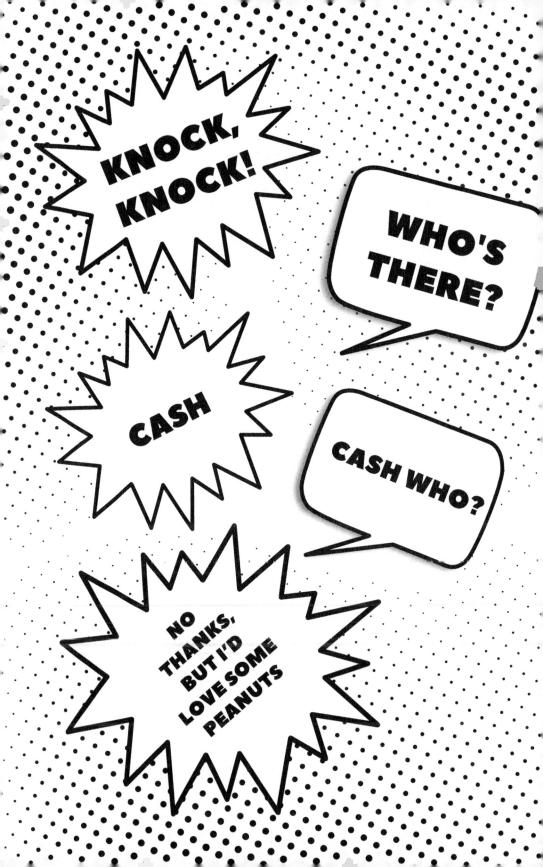

KNOCK, KNOCK!
WHO'S THERE?
EARS
EARS WHO?
'EARS ANOTHER KNOCK KNOCK JOKE FOR YA!

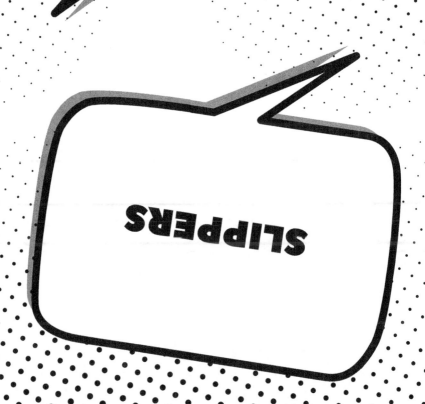

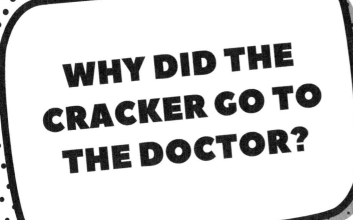

KNOCK, KNOCK!
WHO'S THERE?
ALEX
ALEX WHO?
ALEX-PLAIN LATER, JUST OPEN UP!

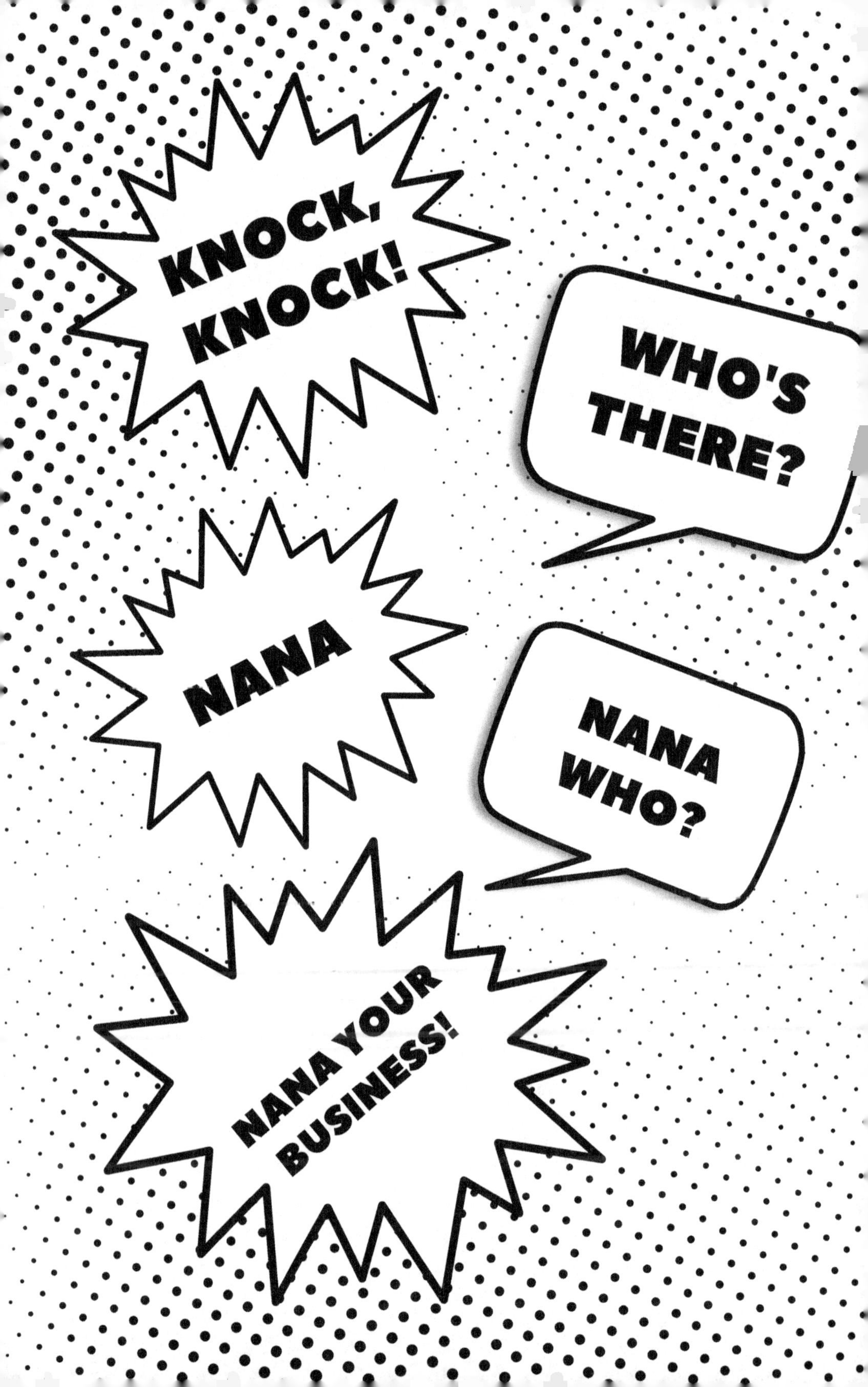
KNOCK, KNOCK!
WHO'S THERE?
NANA
NANA WHO?
NANA YOUR BUSINESS!

FOR CHOOSING OUR SUPER SILLY JOKE BOOK

We know that your time is valuable, and we would be **forever grateful** if you could take a few minutes to leave us your review :)

takes you to your recent purchases on Amazon

www.amazon.com/ryp

Thank you again for your support!

Sincerely,

Diana Keane